MW01712929

Medical Malaprops

Illustrations copyright © 2005 by Jessica Lyn Burhans.

Design: Sally Reed, The Quick Brown Fox, Groton, MA 01450

Published by: Martin & Lawrence Press
37 Nod Road, Box 682
Groton, MA 01450
978/448-6651
www.martinandlawrencepress.com

Publication date: September 2005
Printed in Canada
ISBN 0972168788

Medical Malaprops

TWENTY-FIVE YEARS of GOOD HEALTHY LAUGHS

David Spiegelman, M.D.

MARTIN & LAWRENCE PRESS
GROTON, MASSACHUSETTS

INTRODUCTION

MEDICINE is the only career I ever seriously considered. It has been all I hoped it would be—challenging, stimulating, nurturing, and most importantly, people-centered. I feel fortunate to have had a long-standing connection with a wide variety of people, many of whom are more like family than patients. Secretly, however, I always had a desire to make people laugh. In my youth I spent countless hours listening to the records of Jonathan Winters and Mel Brooks & Carl Reiner and watching W.C. Fields and Marx Brothers movies. I always knew I wasn't clever enough to be funny like they were but wished I could be. I suppose that explains the origin of this collection.

Sometime in 1979 a patient told me she couldn't be pregnant because she had a previous *tubal litigation*. Shortly thereafter another patient related that her *utopian tubes* were blocked. I started taking more notice of these "medical malaprops" and began writing them down so as not to forget them. As my colleagues became aware of this endeavor, they would call me to share amusing things their patients had said or sometimes written. As I shared these with friends and co-workers over the years, the response was uniformly positive. I decided that when the collection grew large enough, I would publish it. While the humor is focused on the language, it seemed that selected malapropisms would be enhanced by illustrations. This has been skillfully accomplished by Jessica Lyn Burhans.

Recent medical research suggests that laughter is good for the cardiovascular system. We already know that it's good for the soul. I hope that this book provides enough laughter to help on both of these accounts.

—DAVID SPIEGELMAN, M.D.

Health Care Access/Funding

Our health care system is rife with problems. Millions of Americans are uninsured and many people have limited access to care. Here are a few innovative methods I have discovered to cope with these problems.

A federal program known as Hill-Burton gives money to hospitals to provide care for those who cannot afford to pay. I had one patient who told me he had *Richard Burton Insurance* and another who presented at the hospital emergency department and told the clerk that he was covered by *Bunker Hill Insurance.*

Another federal program is CHAMPUS. It is a health benefits program for retired military personnel and their dependents. A patient told me he was covered by *Championship Insurance.*

"My old health insurance plan was costing me too much, so I cancelled it and joined HBO."

A patient who had accumulated some bills before she was able to obtain health insurance told me that she was going to have insurance coverage soon and reassured me that it would be *radioactive.*

Many people have heard of the Dartmouth-affiliated Mary Hitchcock Memorial Hospital. A new patient came for an initial visit and told me that her prior medical care was obtained at The *Alfred Hitchcock Clinic.* Similarly, an elderly woman who had been treated at the Leahey Clinic said her care was received at the *Ladies Clinic.*

"I cancelled my health insurance and joined HBO!"
POLICY
HBO

"I went to the hospital yesterday and saw the doctor at the out-going department".

" Well, your office was closed yesterday so I went and saw the doctor at Stop-N-Shop."[1]

Finally there was the patient who went to a walk-in clinic and said he saw *Dr. Ambulatory.*

[1] Health-Stop

The Skin

The skin is actually the largest organ in the body. There are a huge number of diseases that can affect the skin. Here are some unusual ones.

Many people have suffered the pain of a pilonidal cyst. How about a *paranoidal cyst?*

"I saw the dermatologist
and he removed
a subterranean cyst."[2]

An even more exotic type of cyst is the *vivacious cyst.*[3]

[2] subcutaneous

[3] sebaceous

On a health questionnaire a patient wrote that he had previously had an *assist* removed.

Icthyosis is a skin disorder that is not well known to most people. Even fewer know about *ickyosis* (though most of us have felt icky from time-to-time).

A very common skin disorder, eczema, is often seen on the hands. I had a patient with *emphysema* of the hands.

Similarly, acne is extremely common while *ACME* is unusual.

One patient with actinic keratoses on the face told me they were *kinetic keratoses.*

A man asked me to refill his *Rhodesia cream.* It took me a minute to understand that he wanted cream to treat his rosacea.

Speaking of rosacea, a woman requested a refill of the *tropical cream* she was given by her dermatologist.

"The surgeon removed that spot on my leg and told me it was squeamish cell cancer."[4]

A woman with a rash on the skin of her breast said she had *crustaceans*[5] on her nipple.

A young mother told me that she thought her infant's mouth infection was *thrust.*[6]

[4] squamous cell cancer

[5] crusting

[6] thrush

"For the itching, she prescribed
a Tropical cream."

If you are allergic to a medication or a food you may break out in hives, which I have heard called *welches.*[7]

A patient wrote on her health form that she wanted to see a dermatologist to evaluate a *nervous*[8] on her chest.

We don't always have to suture lacerations. Sometimes we can hold the skin edges together with *stereo strips.*[9]

[7] welts

[8] nevus

[9] steri strips

A man who started a new drug for his very extensive psoriasis gleefully proclaimed,

"You know, Doc, my psoriasis improved so much I don't have one psorias."

(This singular vs. plural issue can be confusing. Many people who have had their appendix removed say, "I had them out").

" My mother was diabetic and they had to amputate her leg because of *Gunga-Din*."[10]

[10] gangrene

"I had chest pain during the windmill test."

The Cardiovascular System

Cardiovascular disease remains the leading cause of death in the United States. It is crucial to be informed about cardiovascular problems and the available diagnostic tests and treatments. Here are some of them.

DIAGNOSTIC TESTS

1. Auscultation of the heart by the doctor using a *telescope.*
2. *ZEG* [1]
3. *KGB* [2]
4. *Threadmill* test
5. *Stretch* test
6. *Windmill* test

[1] EKG

[2] EKG (Rusian EKG?)

MALADIES

1. Sprained ankle in the chest[3]
2. *Functioning* heart murmur[4]
3. *Micro valve relapse*[5]
4. *Sleepy* heart attack[6]
5. *Arterial* fibrillation[7]
6. Atrial *aberrations*[8]
7. *Congenital* heart failure[9]
8. *Angiitis* of the heart[10]
9. *Corroded* artery in the neck[11]
10. Bubble on the *aurora*[12]
11. Aneurism on the *menorah*[13]

[3] rarely seen!

[4] functional heart murmur

[5] mitral valve prolapse

[6] silent heart attack

[7] atrial fibrillation

[8] atrial fibrillation

[9] congestive heart failure

[10] angina

[11] carotid artery (which happens to be in the neck)

[12] bubble on the aorta, or aortic aneurism

[13] aorta

TREATMENTS

1. Insertion of a *prostatic* heart valve [14]
2. *Quatriple* bypass [15]
3. Treatment with *dynamite pills* [16]
4. Treatment with *TNT pills* [17]
5. Insertion of a *peacemaker* [18]
6. Placement of a *stench* in the heart [19]

[14] prosthetic heart valve

[15] could this be a 12 vessel bypass?

[16] nitroglycerine

[17] A variation of nitroglycerine—
properly abbreviated TNG (for trinitroglycerine)

[18] pacemaker

[19] stent

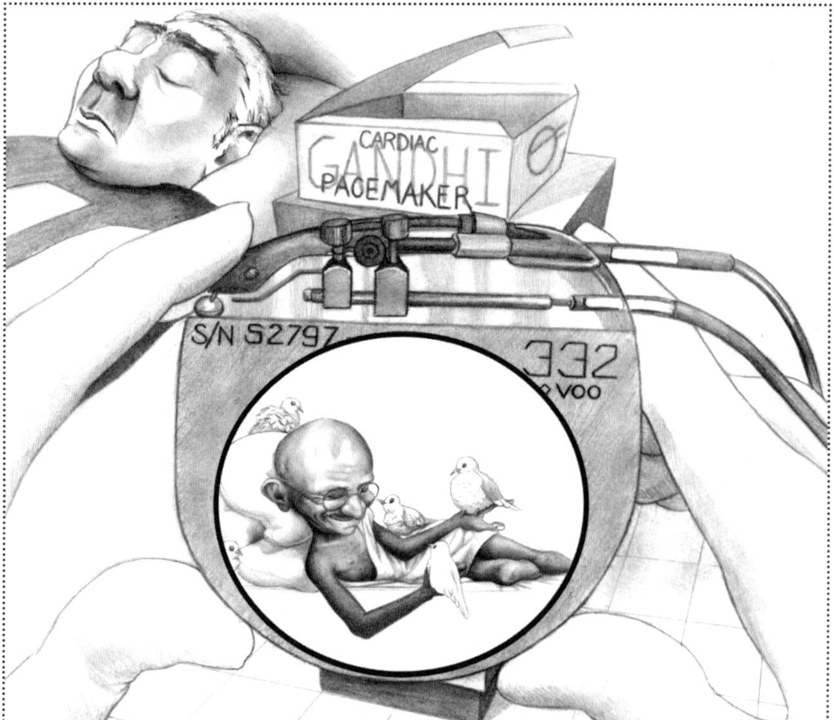

"Because of his slow heart rate, they implanted a peacemaker."

The Gastrointestinal Tract

For me, the expression, "You are what you eat," suggests how important the GI tract is. The digestive tract (or, as I have heard it called, the *indigestive tract*) includes the stomach, intestines, liver, gall bladder, etc. There are many new diagnostic techniques to evaluate this system, some of which are unpleasant.

The trip through the intestinal tract is directed by the GI specialist, the gastroenterologist, also referred to as the *gasologist, gastroneurologist,* or *geniologist.*

"It was terrible.
He kept on hemmorhoiding.[1]"

[1] hemorrhaging (from a hemorrhoid)

Some rare diseases of this system include:

1. *Eternal* hemorrhoids[2]
2. *Gastroneuritis* [3]
3. Esophageal *variouses* [4]
4. *Pollack* in the colon [5]
5. Fecal *compaction* [6]
6. *Cronin's* disease [7]
7. Yellow liver jaundice
8. *Pepsi* ulcer [8]
9. *Calcemized* gall bladder [9]

[2] external (or internal) hemorrhoids

[3] gastroenteritis

[4] esophageal varices

[5] polyps

[6] fecal impaction

[7] Crohn's disease

[8] peptic ulcer

[9] calcified

Most of the diagnostic tests to evaluate the GI tract are associated with some degree of discomfort whether by X-Ray or other method. Here are some of them:

1. *Phase contrast* barium enema[10]
2. *Bavarian* enema
3. *Beryllium* enema

Probably the least favorite exam that people have regularly is the colonoscopy. One patient told me he was having a *colonectomy* (which would actually be a removal of the colon) but the most creative was the *colonostrophy*. This might actually be a preferred name for the procedure since many who have this test consider it a catastrophe.

[10] air contrast barium enema

"...several G.I. tests, including a Bavarian enema."

To prepare for a colonoscopy one must drink a large volume of liquid which has been called *ever-so-lightly*[1]

The tube used to look in the colon is usually called a colonoscope. I have heard 2 much more interesting names used to describe this tube:

1. Kalleidoscope
2. Colossalscope

Looking into the stomach is also performed regularly and the procedure may be called a *gastrosopheny.*[2]

[1] Go-Lytely

[2] Gastroscopy

Hemorrhoids are often painful and can be treated with creams, such as:

1. *Prepatory-H*
2. *Proposition-H*

A surgical procedure performed (more commonly in the past than today) when a condition called portal hypertension exists is a portacaval shunt. A patient once told me that he had a *portable cable shunt.*

HIATAL HERNIA:

This is a very common condition, in which a portion of the stomach pushes up through the opening (hiatus) in the diaphragm. I am aware of no disorder in medicine more confusing to patients than this, as demonstrated by the number of terms used to describe it:

1. Hyannis hernia
2. High test hernia
3. High ass hernia
4. High gas hernia
5. Highlighted hernia
6. Hialeah hernia
7. Hybiscus hernia
8. High terrain hernia
9. Hyenas hernia
10. Hyper hernia

"Is there anything else you can do for an umbiblical hernia?"

There are 2 other rare types of hernias:

1. *Umbiblical* hernia [1]

2. *Bilingual* hernia [2]

Many people were on the Fen-Phen diet a few years ago. I heard about 2 other diets from patients:

1.Flim-flam diet

2. Zen-zen diet

[1] umbilical hernia

[2] inguinal hernia

The Genitourinary System

The genitourinary system is complicated and, for many patients, embarrassing to talk about. It includes the genitalia (which I have heard referred to as the *genitors* or the *gentiles*) as well as the urinary tract. Despite the sometimes sensitive nature of the problems associated with this system, it is important to be able to discuss these matters openly with your physician. Here are some things I have learned from these discussions.

ANATOMY

MALE:

1. *Technicals*
2. *Tentacles*
3. *Intesticles* [1]

[1] It is unclear whether this should be more properly classified as part of the digestive tract

FEMALE:

1. *Utopian* tubes [2]

2. *Crevice* [3]

3. *Bartholomew's* gland [4]

DISEASES

1. *Canada* yeast infection

2. *Cinderella* infection [5]

3. *Prostate* uterus [6]

4. Cervical *displeasure* [7]

[2] fallopian

[3] cervix

[4] Bartholin gland

[5] gardnerella

[6] prolapsed uterus

[7] dysplasia

"Everything was better after the pollack was removed from my colon."

5. Cancer of the *volvo*

6. *Undistended* [8] testicle

7. *Impudence* [9]

8. *Bavarian* cancer [10]

9. *Veterinary* disease [11]

10. *Posteritis* [12]

11. A *noodle* [13] in the prostate

[8] undescended

[9] impotence

[10] ovarian cancer

[11] venereal

[12] prostatitis

[13] nodule

TREATMENTS

1. *Gina Lotrimin* cream [14]
2. *Supranautical* hysterectomy [15]
3. *Catastrophic* hysterectomy [16]
4. *Prospect* operation [17]
5. *Niagra* [18]

[14] gyne lotrimin cream

[15] supracervical hysterectomy

[16] laparoscopic hysterectomy

[17] prostate operation

[18] What a rush!

FAMILY PLANNING OPTIONS

1. *Purpleaptics* [19]
2. *Condiments* [20]
3. *Prophylastics* [21]
4. *Vicectomy* [22]
5. Tubal *litigation* [23]
6. Removal of *production tube*
7. *Corpus* interruptus [24]

[19] prophylactics do come in a variety of colors

[20] there are also flavored condoms

[21] yes, they are stretchy

[22] ouch!

[23] ligation

[24] coitus interruptus

"Her abdominal pain was caused by an atomic pregnancy."

BREAST CANCER DETECTION

1. *Manogram*
2. *Monogram*
3. *Mammulogram*
4. *Mimeogram*

PREGNANCY COMPLICATIONS

1. Placenta *preview* [25]
2. *Atomic* pregnancy [26]
3. *Mist* abortion [27]

[25] placenta previa

[26] ectopic pregnancy

[27] missed abortion

The Neuromuscular System
(including Eye, Ear, Nose, and Throat)

Included here are bones, joints, muscles and the brain and other nerve tissue. Special senses such as sight, smell, as well as psychiatric ailments have been considered here also.

We all know that depression is common. There are several forms of depression and most doctors treat patients for these regularly. Two more difficult to treat forms that I have encountered are *maniac*[1] depression and *double severe* depression.

A man who had a head injury was hospitalized and his wife told me he couldn't be discharged yet because he was having *leisures of the brain*.[2]

[1] manic depression

[2] seizures

Similarly, a patient said that the CAT scan showed that she had two *legions*[3] in her brain.

Head injuries can result in bleeding inside the skull. A patient related that this had happened to her several years before and the diagnosis was a *subzero* hematoma.[4]

"I've just not been myself recently. I'm very jumpy and my nerves are on end."

[3] lesions

[4] subdural hematoma

"I have chronic pain in my back since the surgery. The surgeon told me it was rockenoiditis."[5]

A woman with a tremor came in for a visit. She told me that the tremor had been previously diagnosed. Several members of her family suffered from the same problem. She said she had a *familiar tremor.*[6]

"I had a bad headache last week. It was so bad it was migratin."[7]

This is related to the *mindgraine* headache.

[5] arachnoiditis

[6] familial tremor

[7] migraine

"I've had seizures for years but always know before they happen because I get an aurora."[8]

"I committed suicide three times."

A patient came in with dizziness. He said it happened whenever he stood up and it was accompanied by nausea. He said, "My mother had the same

[8] aura

"I had a heart attack and they put a stench in my heart."

thing and I know what it is." When I asked what he thought it was, he replied, *"vertical sickness."*[9]

The CAT scan didn't explain the back pain so I have to have a milligram." [10]

The varicella-zoster virus causes an eruption in the skin along a single nerve root. It is a reactivation of the same virus that causes chicken pox. It is often painful and is commonly called shingles. I have heard it referred to as *slivers* and *shutters.*

[9] vertigo

[10] myelogram

This one is from a very creative patient. There is an anatomical site in the brain called the centrum semiovale (pronounced semi-oh-valley). This patient referred (in writing) to this site as the *central Seminole valley.*

"He just didn't look right today and when I looked at his eyes his pupils were diluted."[11]

A patient describing his previous medical history said he had a stroke in the *stem cell*[12] of his brain.

"He was confused and having hallusions."[13]

[11] dilated

[12] in the brainstem

[13] hallucinations/delusions

"I have deviated symptoms on the right side." [14]

Two unusual forms of tonsillitis are *subliminal tonsillitis*[15] and *gangoid tonsillitis*[16].

I also have heard of *pustolas*[17] in the throat.

A patient who had a nosebleed saw an ear, nose, and throat specialist and said she had her *corduroys burnt.*[18]

I had one patient tell me he had a *corona*[19] in the eye. Another said she had *arthritis*[20] of the eye.

14 deviated septum to the right side of the nose

15 probably lingual tosillitis

16 probably gangrenous tonsillitis

17 pustules

18 had the bleeding vessel cauterized

19 cornea

20 iritis

Glaucoma is a disease where eye pressures increase and vision declines. Related problems are *blockoma* and *lochloma*.

We all have tear ducts. Someone told me they had *crying tear ducts*.

A man told me he had been treated by an opthalmologist for a *carnal tumor*[21]

A common eye disorder that leads to vision loss is macular degeneration. I have heard it referred to as *immaculate degeneration* on more than one occasion.

Fractures can be all the way through the bone, in which case they are called complete. They also can be

[21] corneal tumor

"I had to have surgery because I had a slippery disc."

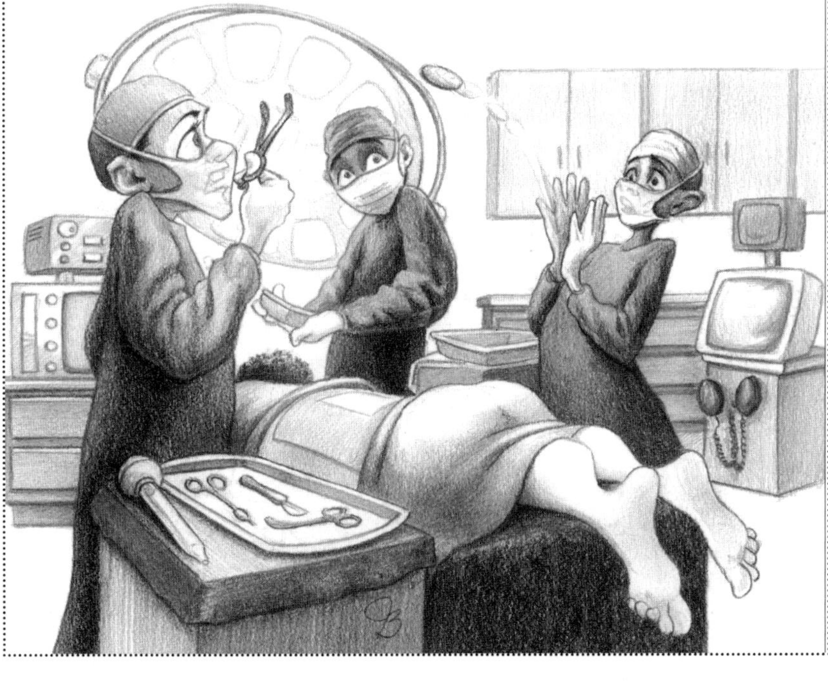

part way through the bone, in which case they are called incomplete, or partial. I once had a patient with an *impartial fracture.*

"I've had a long problem with back pain but two years ago I had to have surgery because I had a *slippery disc.*"[22] (also known occasionally as a *split disc*).

[22] slipped disc

The rotator cuff is a group of tendons (also called *tenements*) that form a cuff around the shoulder joint. It is often referred to as the *rotator cup* or *rotor cup*. I also was once told by a patient that he had a *rotor cap leak*.

"My ligaments were OK but I had a swollen knee cartridge."[23]

[23] cartilage

"I went to the specialist and had some tests which showed a problem with the spinster muscle."[24]

"I woke up this morning and my toe was inflated."[25]

[24] sphincter

[25] inflamed

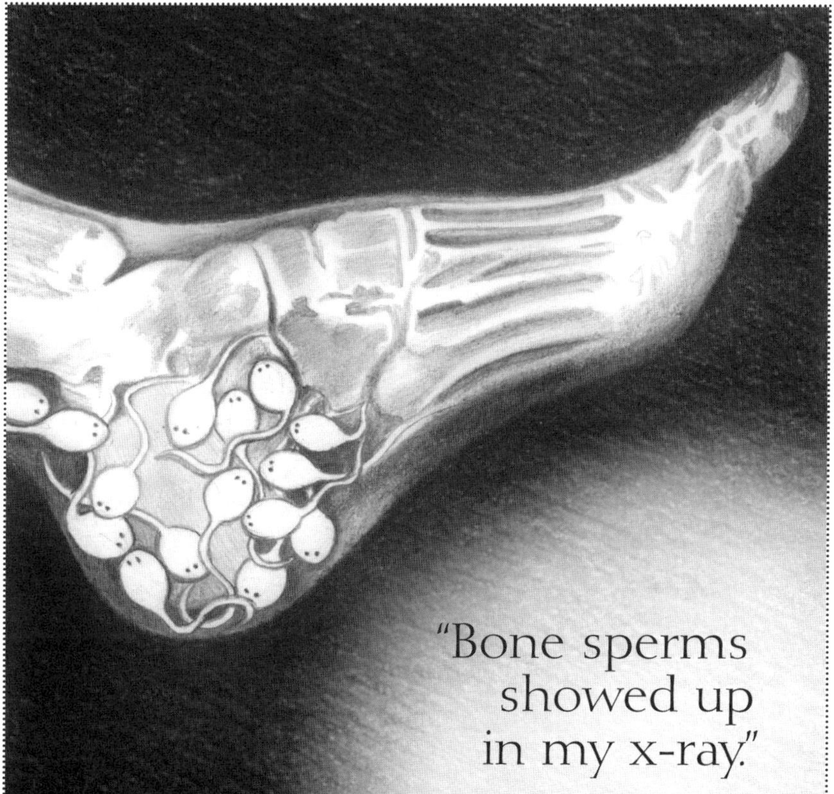
"Bone sperms
showed up
in my x-ray."

"The rheumatologist wasn't sure why my joints were swollen and he did some tests to be sure I don't have a misconnected tissue disease."[26]

If one of these diseases is present it may be treated with an *anti-inflationary*[27] agent.

[26] connective tissue disease

[27] anti-inflammatory

"My shoulder has been hurting. I went to the Emergency Room and they said I had tenderitis."[28]

With aging, the bones may become less dense and be prone to fracture. This condition may be called *Oscar-porosis*.[29]

An adolescent said that he'd not been exercising regularly because he had *Hercules tendonitis*.[30]

[28] tendonitis

[29] osteoporosis

[30] Achilles tendonitis

Remaining Systems

"When I was little I was sick for three months with rudimentary fever."[1]

"It was spider cancer, the kind that goes all over your body."

[1] rheumatic fever

How many people have had the two rare forms of pneumonia listed below?

1. *Brachial* [2] pneumonia
2. *Lobo* [3] pneumonia

"I went to the hospital and the doctor told me I had rapid strep."[4]

[2] bronchial

[3] lobar

[4] strep is a disease; rapid strep is a test to detect the disease

"Dad was in the hospital and became disoriented. They said it was DDTs[5] because of his drinking."

An unusual metabolic disorder is porphyria, Several types exist, one being called porphyria cutanea tarda, which someone referred to as *porphyria tachycardia*.

Neurotic syndrome[6] is not a psychiatric problem but a kidney problem.

An old, and little used name for a type of lung cancer was oat cell cancer. Perhaps its name was changed because patients referred to it as *wheat seed cancer.*

[5] DTs

[6] nephrotic syndrome

"Thank God they sedate you before using the colossalscope."

Here are a few unusual radiologic procedures:

1. *Bean scan*[7]

2. *Casanovagram*[8]

3. *Ultraviolet test*[9]

There are many different forms of anemia. One we probably would all prefer to avoid is *vicious anemia.*[10]

Sometimes, when collecting a urine specimen, we ask patients to provide a mid-stream urine. Someone presented me with a *mid-term urine.*

Is the opposite of hypothermia *heat frustration?*[11]

[7] bone scan

[8] cavernosagram (particularly good since this test is used to evaluate erectile dysfunction)

[9] ultrasound

[10] pernicious anemia

[11] heat prostration

If you sustain a dirty skin wound a tetanus shot is sometimes advised. Has anyone received a *technical* shot?

Just as the EKG can be confusing (see cardiovascular system) so can other abbreviations:

1. VIP [12]
2. MGM [13]
3. MTAs [14]
4. MPs [15]

[12] IVP (x-ray exam of the kidneys)

[13] EMG (electromyogram)

[14] EMTs

[15] EMTs

Not Nessarily Medical,
though sometimes related

"I know my cholesterol will be high because we went out to dinner last night and I had Lobster Newburyport."

"What we need right now is an intrusion of funds to save Social Security."

"If people find out about this
it could do irreputable damage
to my reputation."

"My dog just died. It was
a mix between a poodle
and a lapso."

"I'm very worried about
the future of our climate
on this planet.
It's a global warning."

"This situation was worsening quickly. I wanted to bite this in the bullet before it got out of hand."

"He had a big argument with her and they went neck-and-neck."

"It's all happening to me at once, the whole ten yards."

"So we tried that Y-2K jelly..."

"Whenever I get a headache stress irgs it on."

"Whenever I take antihistamines, I get very droggy."

"She stayed with that man way too long. I told her not to put all her eggs in one bastard."

"That's how I felt deep down, to basic brass roots"

"It's too late now,
the cat's out of the barn."

"He got a new dog.
It's a borderline collie."

"This was not my idea.
All along I was
diabolically opposed to it."

"I never behaved that way.
It's just not my bag of tea."

"It was one of those shaggy
little dogs, an ipso-lapso."

"I think he did it because he was trying to get his name in the McGinnis Book of World Records."

"I saw that doctor you recommended but quite frankly, I was not too infused about him."

"I thought I was getting a cold, so I went to the health food store for euthanesia."

Potpourri of Patient Quotations

I advised an alcoholic patient that if he didn't stop drinking he would die of liver failure. He was able to quit and after several months of sobriety I congratulated him. He lamented that he was having trouble getting women to go out with him because he wasn't drinking, and proclaimed, "For God's sake, Doc, I'm leading a *celebrity* life!"

Another man tried to excuse his alcohol abuse and said, "I'm only drinking for *municipal* purposes."

"I saw the dermatologist
and he removed a mole and
it was a ligament."[1]

"He spoke at the meeting
and people liked him
so much they gave him
a standing ovulation."

[1] malignant

"I'll do whatever you say. You're the doctor and I'm the patron."

"I had a bad cold so I went to the health food store and got euthanasia."[2]

[2] echinacea

"There was a fire and he inhaled
so much smoke
he got sophisticated."

In discussing end-of-life issues with an elderly woman she related the following wish to me.

"Whatever happens,
I don't want to end up
like an animal."

"As soon as the ambulance got to the hospital, they x-rated me."

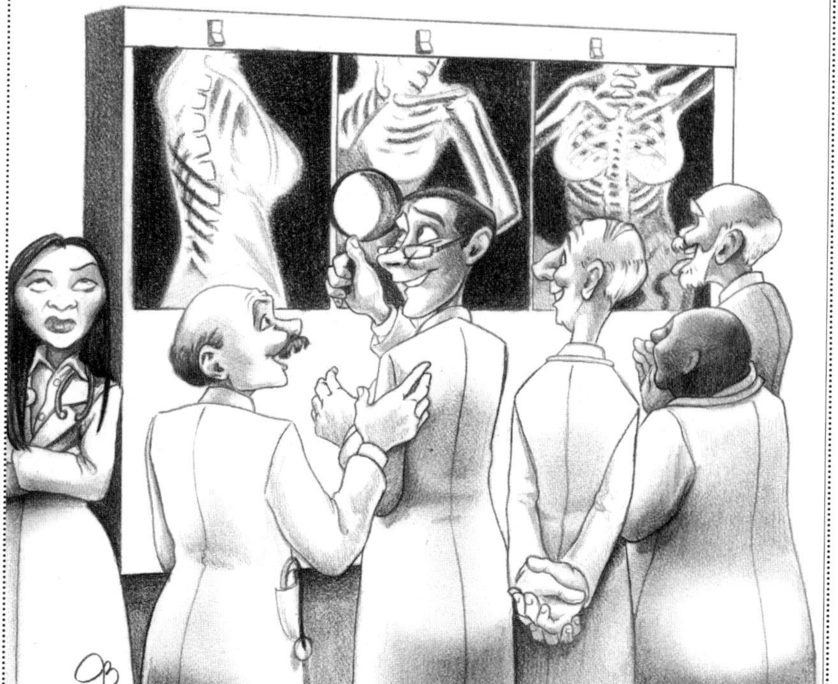

In another conversation about end-of-life care a man said about his wife, who was suffering from respiratory problems,

"I don't know if she wants to be incubated."[3]

"I saw the eye doctor and he fixed the problem with a razor beam."

[3] intubated

A woman was concerned about her father's weight loss and said,

"He's not eating much and he's starting to get emancipated."

An elderly patient was having problems with confusion. Her daughter said,

"She gets disoriental and is having disillusions."

"Dad's losing his memory so we had to go to a lawyer and get power of eternity."

"I was coughing so hard I was wrenching over the toilet."

"My brother had a tumor but thank God it was malignant."

A man was relating the events of his recent consult with a neurologist. I asked him what the neurologist did and he said,

"He checked me for reflections."[4]

[4] reflexes

"The flight wasn't bad at all...
the paraplegics were so
kind to me."

A patient who had been vomiting said,

"I don't know why I'm throwing up, I didn't eat anything erotic."

A man went to the emergency department and had to be transferred to another hospital urgently by helicopter. When asked about the trip he said,

"It was fine because the paraplegics in the helicopter were so nice to me."

"I went to the emergency room and got X-rated."

A man told me his cough was very bad and he was

"...coughing up sperm."[5]

An elderly patient was confused and her daughter said,

"She has not been too cohesive."

[5] sputum

A patient who was describing the treatment he had for a rash said,

"The only thing that helped was when they gave me 30 grams of chromosomes."[6]

A man told me about a trip to the hospital for emergency treatment of a breathing problem and said,

"They put a cathode[7] in my nose to give me oxygen."

[6] cortisone

[7] catheter

A woman who was describing her irregular menstrual periods stated that her periods were *"radical."*

A patient was describing her recent hospitalization and said,

"They said I couldn't be discharged from the hospital till my autopsy report was back."

On a written health history form a patient wrote that his mother *died of "childhood."*

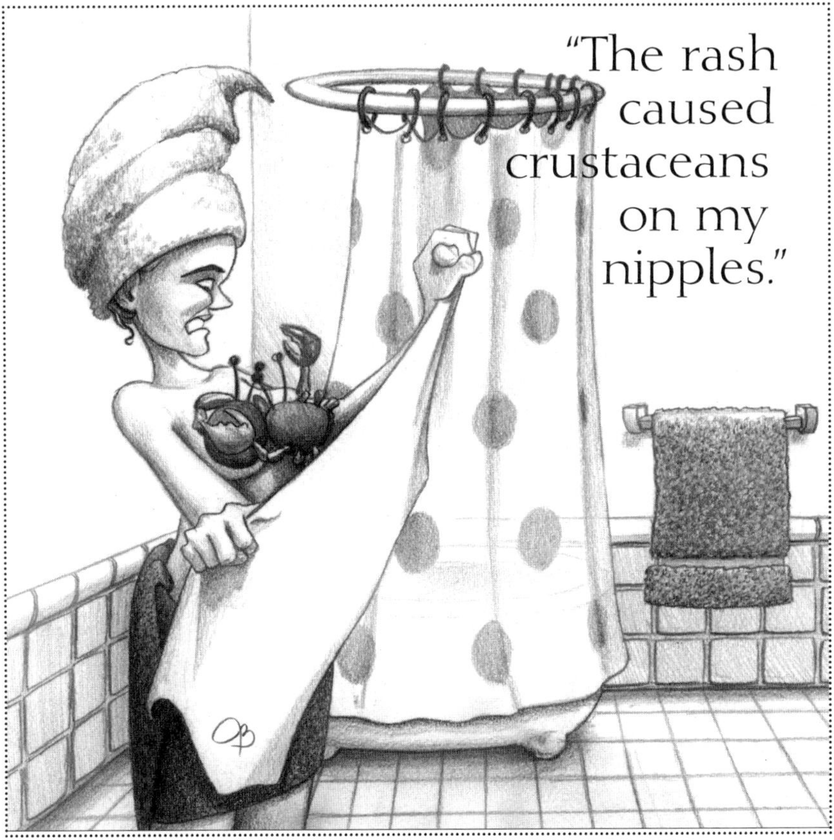
"The rash caused crustaceans on my nipples."

Another written health questionnaire asked about family history and someone wrote that their father had undergone a *"baloney amputation."*[8]

"I was doing a lot of lifting and overstrenuated myself."

A patient was describing the results of a neurologic problem and said the previous doctor told her,

"Your nerves are very inflammable."

[8] below the knee

A man was describing how lethargic his father was and said,

"He was moving very slow and laxative."[9]

"I was vomiting so much I got hydrated."

[9] lackadaisical

"I went on vacation and got so constipated I had to be unpacked." [10]

"They had to admit him to the hospital because his electrodes were down."[11]

[10] disimpacted (this has nothing to do with your luggage)

[11] electrolytes

"I was so hungry I started to gouge myself."

"I really didn't have any pain after the surgery because they gave me an epidermal."[12]

[12] epidural

"They said I had a problem with my limp nose."

"For a while they couldn't figure out what was wrong with me but eventually they decided it was my limp nose."[13]

"He was outside in the cold so long he was suffering from hypodermia."[14]

"Why does my husband wheezle?"[15]

13 lymph nodes

14 hypothermia

15 wheeze

"So many people in my family have had heart problems—I think it's genital."[16]

A patient having problems with constipation said,

"I was so badly constipated I had to take a physical."[17]

[16] congenital

[17] physic

"Doctor, I just can't lose weight on my own. Can't you give me something to curve my appetite?"

A patient went in for some tests before his upcoming surgery and said, "I just had my *preopsy.*"

"My Mom's kidneys are failing. Now, in addition to everything else, she has to go three times a week for electrolysis."[18]

[18] dialysis

When asked how they were feeling one patient responded, *"Fair to Middleton"* and another, *"Matzo-matzo."* Yet another said he was fatigued and didn't have any *"zesto."*

In addition to the woman who was *"deaf-as-a-bat"* there was one who was *"weak-as-a-chicken"* and another who was *"happy-as-a-lamb."*

"It was horrible. The pain was inscrutiating."

"They told me that the therapy was not going to be a pancreas." [19]

[19] panacea

"How do I feel?
Oh . . . just
matzo-matzo."

"I couldn't send him to that school because the bathroom there smelled so strong of pneumonia that it nearly choked me."

"I saw that urologist you recommended and he checked me with a dictoscope."[20]

[20]cystoscope

Medications

Whoever creates medication names has little regard for the average patient. Getting these names right can be very difficult. The following examples illustrate how difficult it can be.

1. Alaprazam (pronounced al-a-pra-ZAM) (alprazolam)
2. Ivyprophen (ibuprophen)
3. Tylenol depository (Tylenol suppository)
4. Ethnic aspirin (enteric coated aspirin)
5. Elastic (lasix)
6. Latex (lasix)
7. Progresso (lopressor)

8. Aristocrat ointment (aristocort ointment)

9. I-bufferin (ibuprophen)

10. I.B. prophen (ibuprophen)

11. Neptune (neptazine)

12. Thermidor (theodur)

13. Revlon (reglan)

14. Feverbarbital (phenobarbital)

15. Frolic acid (folic acid)

16. Provincial (proventil)

17. Quisine (quinidine)

18. Howard Johnson aspirin
(Johnson & Johnson aspirin)

19. Rose heparin (rocephin)

20. Celebrant (celebrex)

21. Metamusical (metamucil)

21. Impramine (imipramine)

22. Valiants (valiums)

23. Pepso-Bismark (Pepto-Bismol)

24. Xanthrax (any comination of zantac, xanax, zithromax, and anthrax)

25. Dioxaclean (doxycycline)

26. Doctorcillin (doxycycline)

27. Sodium menthol (sodium pentathol)

28. Protocol (pravachol)

HOWARD
JOHNSON'S
Pain Relief
small...
med...
FLAVORS
"I take Howard Johnson Aspirin."

Acknowledgements

I've amused myself by thinking about this project for years but probably would never have completed it without the encouragement and help of Sally Reed. Her sound advice, keen visual sense, and wonderful sense of humor were invaluable. She is one of those rare people who knows a lot about everything and has an irresistible laugh to boot.

I also want to thank my colleagues who always notified me about their patients' "contributions" to this collection — especially Drs. Richard Schwartz, Gary Asher, Ken Janes, George Geibel, and Paul Foster.

Mostly, thanks to all the people who have trusted me to provide their health care over the last twenty-seven years. We've shared joy, grief, good times and bad. I hope this book allows us to share a laugh.

—David Spiegelman, M.D.

Got a favorite

Medical Malaprop

of your own?

Visit www.medicalmalaprops.com

and contribute it

to the next collection.